Whitman
and Truth

First published in the United Kingdom in 2022 by
Shearsman Books
PO Box 4239
Swindon
SN3 9FN

Shearsman Books Ltd Registered Office
30–31 St. James Place, Mangotsfield, Bristol BS16 9JB
(this address not for correspondence)

www.shearsman.com

ISBN 978-1-84861-792-6

Whitman
and Truth

J.H. Prynne

Shearsman Books

POETRY AND TRUTH
An Example from Whitman

A March in the Ranks Hard-Prest, and the Road Unknown

A march in the ranks hard-prest, and the road unknown,
A route through a heavy wood with muffled steps in the darkness,
Our army foil'd with loss severe, and the sullen remnant retreating,
Till after midnight glimmer upon us the lights of a dim-lighted building,
We come to an open space in the woods, and halt by the dim-lighted
      building,
'Tis a large old church at the crossing roads, now an impromptu hospital,
Entering but for a minute I see a sight beyond all the pictures and
      poems ever made,
Shadows of deepest, deepest black, just lit by moving candles and lamps,
And by one great pitchy torch stationary with wild red flame and clouds
      of smoke,
By these, crowds, groups of forms vaguely I see on the floor, some in
      the pews laid down,
At my feet more distinctly a soldier, a mere lad, in danger of bleeding to
      death, (he is shot in the abdomen),
I stanch the blood temporarily, (the youngster's face is white as a lily,)
Then before I depart I sweep my eyes, o'er the scene fain to absorb it all,
Faces, varieties, postures beyond description, most in obscurity, some
      of them dead,
Surgeons operating, attendants holding lights, the smell of ether, the
      odor of blood, The crowd, O the crowd of the bloody forms,
      the yard outside also fill'd,
Some on the bare ground, some on planks or stretchers, some in the
      death-spasm sweating,
An occasional scream or cry, the doctor's shouted orders or calls,
The glisten of the little steel instruments catching the glint of the torches,
These I resume as I chant, I see again the forms, I smell the odor,
Then hear outside the orders given, *Fall in, my men, fall in;*
But first I bend to the dying lad, his eyes open, a half-smile gives he me,

Then the eyes close, calmly close, and I speed forth to the darkness,
Resuming, marching, ever in darkness marching, on in the ranks,
The unknown road still marching.

WALT WHITMAN (1819–1892), from *Drum-Taps* (1865), a collection
of poems written in response to the American Civil War (1861–65)
and privately printed by the author; incorporated into the 4th edition of his *Leaves of Grass* (1867). Full text given in Justin Kaplan
(ed.), *Walt Whitman, Complete Poetry and Collected Prose* (Library of
America, New York, NY, 1982), pp. 439–40, and also conveniently
available in Francis Murphy (ed.), *Walt Whitman, The Complete Poems*
(Penguin Books, London, 1975 and reprinted), pp. 330–31. An editor
of the *Drum-Taps* volume in facsimile has given his opinion that 'it
is the greatest book of war lyrics ever written by a single author'—F.
DeWolfe Miller (ed.), *Walt Whitman's Drum-Taps (1865) and Sequel to
Drum-Taps (1865–6)* (Gainesville, FL, 1959), p. viii. In this narrative,
derived from the Battle of White Oak Swamp (30th June 1862, see
below), the 'mere lad' is brought in from, or transfers into, Whitman's
account of the Battle of Chancellorsville, 30th April–6th May 1863 (in
his *Memoranda During the War,* later in *Specimen Days,* also see below).

In the original printing of *Drum-Taps,* over which Whitman exercised
close practical supervision, the long verse lines in this poem (pp. 44–
5), as in many others, could mostly not be fitted unbroken into the
page format; all but the first and last (shorter) lines were broken, with
justified left and right margin, and even the first line as title (centred)
took up two lines. One, the longest line of all, took up three lines of
type, and was broken by a hyphen (the only such hyphen), thus:

> At my feet more distinctly a soldier, a mere lad, in
> > danger of bleeding to death, (he is shot in the abdo-
> > men;)

The alert reader will notice that a small sharp piece of metal (the piece
of type bearing the hyphen, made of lead like a bullet) has broken into
the body of the word (the medical, not commonplace word) for this
soldier's stomach, just where the enemy bullet has inflicted the death-
wound.

1. It *[Drum-Taps]* is in my opinion superior to *Leaves of Grass* – certainly more perfect as a work of art, being adjusted in all its proportions, & its passion having the indispensable merit that though to the ordinary reader let loose with wildest abandon, the true artist can see that it is yet under control. But I am perhaps mainly satisfied with *Drum-Taps* because it delivers my ambition of the task that has haunted me, namely, to express in a poem (& in the way I like, which is not at all by directly stating it), the pending action of this *Time & Land we swim in,* with all their large conflicting fluctuations of despair & hope, the shiftings, masses, & the whirl & deafening din, (yet over all, as by invisible hand, a definite purport & idea) – with the unprecedented anguish of wounded & suffering, the beautiful young men, in wholesale death & agony, everything sometimes as if in blood color, & dripping blood. The book is therefore unprecedentedly sad (as these days are, are they not?) – but it also has the blast of the trumpet, & the drum pounds & whirrs in it, & then an undertone of sweetest comradeship & human love, threading its steady thread inside the chaos, & heard at every lull & interstice thereof. Truly also it has clear notes of faith & triumph.

WALT WHITMAN, from a letter to William D. O'Connor dated 6th January 1865, during the period when he was frustratedly seeking a publisher for this book while at the same time planning to have it privately printed (F. DeWolfe Miller [ed.], *Walt Whitman's 'Drum-Taps' (1865) and 'Sequel to Drum-Taps' (1865–6)* [facsimile], ed. F. DeWolfe Miller (Gainesville, FL, 1959, reprinted 1979), pp. xxvi–ix). Text from Walt Whitman, *The Correspondence,* Vol. 1: 1842–1867, ed. Edwin Haviland Miller (New York, NY, 1961), pp. 246–7; and see Roy Morris, Jr, *The Better Angel; Walt Whitman in the Civil War* (Oxford, 2000), pp. 217–8.

2. Without effort and without exposing in the least how it is done the greatest poet brings the spirit of any or all events and passions and scenes and persons some more and some less to bear on your individual character as you hear or read. To do this well is to compete with the laws that pursue and follow time. What is the purpose must surely be there and the clue of it must be there ... and the faintest indication is the indication of the best and then becomes the clearest indication. Past and present and future are not disjoined but joined.

The great poets are also to be known by the absence in them of tricks and by the justification of perfect personal candor. Then folks echo a new cheap joy and a divine voice leaping from their brains: How beautiful is candor! All faults may be forgiven of him who has perfect candor. Henceforth let no man of us lie, for we have seen that openness wins the inner and outer world and that there is no single exception, and that never since our earth gathered itself into a mass have deceit or subterfuge or prevarication attracted its smallest particle or the faintest tinge of a shade—and that through the enveloping wealth and rank of a state or the whole republic of states a sneak or sly person shall be discovered and despised ... and that the soul has never been once fooled and never can be fooled ... and thrift without the loving nod of the soul is only a foetid puff ... and there never grew up in any of the continents of the globe [...] a being whose instinct hated the truth.

WALT WHITMAN, from the Preface to *Leaves of Grass* (1855); text from Justin Kaplan (ed.), *Walt Whitman, Complete Poetry and Collected Prose* (Library of America, New York, NY, 1982), pp. 12–13; 19–20. The word 'cheap' here is not used disapprovingly but to describe that which is inexpensive and affordable by ordinary people. The four full-stops in brackets indicate that a passage in the original text has been omitted; the four full-stops not placed in brackets were inserted by the author and do not mark an omission. Full text of the Preface is also included in Francis Murphy's edition. For the earlier history of 'candour' in British/ English usage see William Empson, *The Structure of Complex Words* (3rd ed., London, 1977), chap. 15, and Donald Davie, 'An Episode in the History of Candour' in his *Dissentient Voice* (Notre Dame, IN, 1982).

3. **Witness,** *n.* 1. Attestation of a fact or an event; testimony. 2. That which furnishes evidence or proof. 3. One who is cognizant; a person who beholds, or otherwise has personal knowledge of, anything; as, an eye*witness;* an ear*witness.*

Witness, *v. t.* 1. To see or know by personal presence; to have direct cognizance of.

Webster's International Dictionary of the English Language; being the authentic edition of Webster's Unabridged Dictionary, comprising the issues of 1864, 1879, and 1884, thoroughly revised... (Springfield, MA, 1903).

4. Scene in the woods on the Peninsula—told me by Milton Roberts Ward G (Maine).

After the battle of White Oaks Church, on the retreat, the march at night – the scene between 12 & 2 o'clock that night. at the church in the woods, the hospital show at night, the wounded brought in – previous, the silent stealthy march through the woods, at times stumbling over the bodies of dead men in the road (there had been terrible fighting there that day, only closing at dark—we retreating the artillery horses feet muffled, orders that men should tread light & only speak in whispers –

Then between midnight & 1 o'clock we halted to rest a couple of hours at an opening in the woods – in this opening was a pretty good sized old church used impromptu for a hospital for the wounded of the battles of the day thereabout – with these it was filled, all varieties horrible beyond description – the darkness dimly lit with candles, lamps torches, moving about, but plenty of darkness & half darkness, – the crowds of wounded, bloody & pale, the surgeons operating – the yards outside also filled – they lay on the ground, some on blankets, some on stray planks, – the despairing screams & curses of some out of their senses, the murky darkness, the gleaming of the torches, the smoke from them too, the doctors operating, the scent of chloroform, the glisten of the steel instruments as the flash of lamps fell upon them.

WALT WHITMAN, manuscript war-hospital notebook entry, dated to June–July 1863, of which now only four photocopied pages survive (Library of Congress, Washington). Milton Roberts was a badly wounded soldier whom Whitman visited in the Armoury Square Hospital (Washington) and who described this battle scene to Whitman, who wrote down these notes as Roberts briefly told his story. Text here from Walt Whitman, *Notebooks and Unpublished Prose Manuscripts*, ed. Edward F. Grier, Vol. II: Washington (New York, 1984), pp. 651–2. For the connection with Whitman's poem see Mark Maslan, *Whitman Possessed; Poetry, Sexuality, and Popular Authority* (Baltimore, MD, 2001), pp. 118–36, and, in less detail, Timothy Sweet, *Traces of War; Poetry, Photography, and the Crisis of the Union* (Baltimore, MD, 1990), pp. 37–45.

The Battle of White Oak Swamp took place on 30th June 1862, part of the Seven Days Battles in the American Civil War, fought in Henrico County, Virginia. As the Union (i.e. Northern) Army of the Potomac retreated southeast towards the James River, its rearguard under Major-General William B. Franklin blocked off the advance of Major-General Thomas J. 'Stonewall' Jackson's divisions at the White Oak Bridge Crossing, resulting in an artillery duel. These running battles incurred major loss of life: 15,000 Union soldiers died during the retreat. But Jackson was thus prevented from joining the consolidated assault on the Union Army that had been ordered by General Robert E. Lee, Commander of the Confederate (i.e. Southern) Armies, producing an inconclusive result at Glendale, but one in which the Union Army avoided destruction. These seven days, which included the night-time retreat through the White Oaks woods and swamps, were a confused and complex chain of fighting encounters, with many dying and little clear advantage gained on either side.

5. *May 12* [1863) – A *Night Battle, over a week since.* – *We* already talk of Histories of the War, (presently to accumulate) – yes – technical histories of some things, statistics, official reports, and so on – but shall we ever get histories of the *real* things? ...... There was part of the late battle at Chancellorsville, (second Fredericksburgh,) a little over a week ago, Saturday, Saturday night and Sunday, under Gen. Joe Hooker, I would like to give just a glimpse of – (a moment's look in a terrible storm at sea – of which a few suggestions are enough, and full details impossible.) [...]. It was the tug of Saturday evening, and through the night and Sunday morning, I wanted to make a special note of. It was largely in the woods, and quite a general engagement. The night was very pleasant, at times the moon shining out full and clear, all Nature so calm in itself, the early summer grass so rich, and foliage of the trees – yet there the battle raging, and many good fellows lying helpless, with new accessions to them, and every minute amid the rattle of muskets and crash of cannon, (for there was an artillery contest too,) the red life-blood oozing out from heads or trunks or limbs upon that green and dew-cool grass.

There they lie, in the largest [camp of the wounded], in an open space in the woods, from 500 to 600 poor fellows – the groans and screams – the odor of blood, mixed with the fresh scent of the night [...]. Some have their legs blown off-some bullets through the breast – some indescribably horrid wounds in the face or head, all mutilated, sickening, torn, gouged out – some in the abdomen – some mere boys – here is one his face colorless as chalk, lying perfectly still, a bullet has perforated the abdomen—life is ebbing fast, there is no help for him. In the camp of the wounded are many rebels, badly hurt – they take their regular turns with the rest, just the same as any – the surgeons use them the same.

Such, amid the woods, that scene of flitting souls – amid the crack and crash and yelling sounds – the impalpable perfume of the woods—and yet the pungent, stifling smoke –

shed with the radiance of the moon, the round, maternal queen, looking from heaven at intervals so placid – the sky so heavenly – the clear-obscure up there, those buoyant upper oceans – a few large placid stars beyond, coming out and then disappearing – the melancholy, draperied night above, around......And there, upon the roads, the fields, and in those woods, that contest, never one more desperate in any age or land – both parties now in force – masses – no fancy battle, no semi-play, but fierce and savage demons fighting there—courage and scorn of death the rule, exceptions almost none.

WALT WHITMAN, from *Memoranda During the War [&] Death of Abraham Lincoln* [facsimile reprint], ed. Roy P. Basler (Bloomington, IN, 1962), pp. 13, 14–15. The full-stops in brackets indicate that a passage in the original text has been omitted; the multiple full-stops not placed in brackets were inserted by the author and do not mark an omission. 'Rebels' is an usual name for soldiers (also 'secesh', for secessionist) from the Confederate (i.e. southern) armies. This collection of reports and diaries was planned out by October 1863 but not finally published until 1875; the editor comments: 'Of course, Whitman was not an eyewitness of every incident or scene which he included in *Memoranda During the War*. For the writing of those he did not witness, he went about collecting his material just as any good reporter or historian would' (p. [23]; see also Justin Kaplan, *Walt Whitman; A Life* [New York, 1980]. pp. 277–8). Many early passages in this collection are later incorporated into *Specimen Days and Collect* (1882), including the excerpts given here; see *Complete Poetry and Collected Prose,* ed. Kaplan (New York, 1962), pp. 721–4. At the Battle of Chancellorsville (30th April–6th May 1863) General Robert E. Lee defeated a substantially superior Union force; at the peak of the fighting on 3rd May about 18,000 men died in battle, divided equally between both sides.

6. These Hospitals, so different from all others – these thousands, and tens and twenties of thousands of American young men, badly wounded, all sorts of wounds, operated on, pallid with diarrhea, languishing, dying with fever, pneumonia, &c. open a new world somehow to me, giving closer insights, new things, exploring deeper mines than any yet, showing our humanity, (I sometimes put myself in fancy in the cot, with typhoid, or under the knife,) tried by terrible, fearfulest tests, probed deepest, the living soul's, the body's tragedies, bursting the petty bonds of art. To these, what are your dramas and poems, even the oldest and tearfulest? Not old Greek mighty ones, where man contends with fate, (and always yields) – not Virgil showing Dante on and on among the agonized & damned, approach what here I see and take a part in. For here I see, not at intervals, but quite always, how certain, man, our American man – how he holds himself cool and unquestioned master above all pains and bloody mutilations. It is immense, the best thing of all, nourishes me of all men.

WALT WHITMAN, from a letter to Nathaniel Bloom and John F.S. Gray dated 19th March 1863, written from Washington after his return from the battle zone and the commencement of his regular hospital visits; *Correspondence,* Vol. 1:1842–1867, ed. Edwin Haviland Miller (New York, 1961), pp. 81–22; and see Roy Morris, Jr, *The Better Angel; Walt Whitman in the Civil War* (Oxford, 2000), pp. 217–8.

7. Another corpse was that of a youth, perhaps eighteen years old, fair-haired, rough chinned. He was lying in the snow on his back, staring at the blue day with eyes as blue and icy; his feet were towards the German lines, and his right hand clutched the wooden handle of a bomb.

EDMUND BLUNDEN, from *Undertones of War,* his trench memoir of the Great War of 1914–18; Blunden is recalling his patrol of the English front line during which he comes across these German casualties killed during the raid of the previous night *(Undertones of War* [London, 1928], p. 173). The scene is the Somme Offensive of winter 1916, but this account is constructed in deep retrospect, from twelve years later. In his Preliminary foreword Blunden comments that 'distancing memory' made the task of narrative hard to manage, and yet the distance was needed in order to achieve perspective and control. Chapter XVI is titled 'A German Performance', suggesting an ironic parody of theatrical entertainment, another distancing device. The dead boy described here is a German, with typically fair hair and blue eyes, and thus generically 'the enemy'; but there is no hostile attitude, the mention of him is neutral in tone and quite detached (see Barry Webb, *Edmund Blunden; A Biography* [New Haven, CT, 1990], p. 93).

8. Grandad staggered down the road, weaving in and out of the sorghum field on the western edge, Father right on his heels. They stepped on broken, twisted stalks of sorghum and spent cartridges that gave off a faint yellow glint. Frequently they bent down to look at the bodies of their fallen comrades, who lay amid the sorghum, deathly grimaces frozen on their faces. Granddad and Father shook them in hope of finding one who was alive; but they were dead, all of them. Father's and Granddad's hands were covered with sticky blood. Father looked down at two soldiers on the western-most edge of the field: one lay with the muzzle of his shotgun in his mouth, the back of his neck a gory mess, like a rotten wasps' nest; the other lay across a bayonet buried in his chest. When Granddad turned them over, Father saw that their legs had been broken and their bellies slit open. Granddad sighed as he withdrew the shotgun from the one soldier's mouth and pulled the bayonet from the other's chest.

The torchbearers fell in behind Granddad and Father, the flames lighting up the blurry riverbed and the sorghum fields all the way up to the battleground near the bridge. The burned-out trucks cast eerie shadows. Corpses strewn across the battlefield gave off an overpowering stench of blood, which merged with the smell of scorched metal, of the sorghum that served as a vast backdrop, and of the river so far from its source.

Women began to wail as drops of burning oil fell from the torches onto the people's hands and feet. The men's faces looked like steel fresh from the furnace. The white stone bridge had turned scarlet.

MO YAN (GUAN MO-YE, born 1955), from *Red Sorghum (Hong Gao Liang)* (1987), Book 2 chap. 3, chap. 7, trans. Howard Goldblatt from the Taipei Hong-fan Book Co. ed. of 1988, with corrections and deletions as approved by the author. Text here from the London (Heinemann) ed. of 1993, pp. 100, 140. This village ambush against an armed convoy of the occupying Japanese forces is placed historically in the autumn of 1939. The Chinese 'Fifth Generation' film-maker Zhang Yimou made *Red Sorghum (Hong Gaoliang,* 1987) as his first movie, adapted from the first two parts of the novel; see Jerome Silbergeld, *China into Film; Frames of Reference in Contemporary Chinese Cinema* (London, 1999), Chap. 2: 'Ruins of a Sorghum Field, Eclipse of a Nation: *Red Sorghum* on Page and Screen' (pp. 53–95); also Yingjin Zhang, *Chinese National Cinema* (New York, 2004), pp. 235–40 ('fabricated history as myth', p. 238).

9. Throughout much of its length, the film glows with the colour red-pink in its few happy moments, fiery red or blood red when the temperature heats up. Jiu'er herself is the fiercest, reddest soul of all. Unlike *Yellow Earth's* Cuiqiao, she's hardly a child bride and more than a match for her two mates, two facts that may stretch credibility sociologically but which, with Gu Changwei's bold cinematography and Zhang Yimou's taut directorial management, contribute to a mythic story-telling effect. To the shock (and fascination) of Chinese audiences, *Red Sorghum* substituted a realistically brutal visualization for the artificially staged pseudo-toughness of socialist film-making.

JEROME SILBERGELD, op. cit., p. 57. For a more sceptical view see MingBao Yue, "Visual Agency and Ideological Fantasy in Three Films by Zhang Yimou" in *Narratives of Agency; Self-Making in China, India, and Japan* (Minneapolis, MN, 1996), Chap. 3 (pp. 56–73): "…despite empathy with the tragedy displayed on the screen, the viewer is ultimately unable to evade the seductive powers of Zhang's artistic study of the image. In this way, the use of col or and sound is allowed to overpower the much more oppressive aspects…[11] (p. 57). For an overview see also Xudong Zhang, *Chinese Modernism in the Era of Reforms; Cultural Fever, AvantGarde Fiction, and the New Chinese Cinema* (Durham, NC, 1997), Chap. 11: "Ideology and Utopia in Zhang Yimou's *Red Sorghum*" (pp, 306–28).

10. *Of course* the tumult of a battle is grand, the results of a battle tragic, and the untimely deaths of young men a theme for elegies. But he is not a poet who merely reiterates these plain facts *ore rotunda* [in a grand voice]. He only sings them worthily who views them from a height. Every tragic event collects about it a number of persons who delight to dwell upon its superficial points—of minds which are bullied by the *accidents* of the affair. The temper of such minds seems to us to be the reverse of the poetic temper; for the poet, although he incidentally masters, grasps, and uses the superficial traits of his theme, is really a poet only in so far as he extracts its latent meaning and holds it up to common eyes.

To sing aright our battles and our glories it is not enough to have served in a hospital (however praiseworthy the task in itself), to be aggressively careless, inelegant, and ignorant, and to be constantly preoccupied with yourself. You must also be serious. You must forget yourself in your ideas. Your personal qualities—the vigor of your temperament, the manly independence of your nature, the tenderness of your heart—these facts are impertinent. You must be *possessed,* and you must strive to possess your possession. If in your striving you break into divine eloquence, then you are a poet. If the idea which possesses you is the idea of your country's greatness, then you are a national poet; and not otherwise.

[HENRY JAMES], from 'Mr. Walt Whitman', anonymous review of *Drum-Taps,* in *The Nation* for 16th November 1965 (when James was 22); in later life James condemned this review as produced 'in the gross impudence of youth'. Text from Leon Edel (ed.), *Henry James; The American Essays* (New York, 1956, reprinted, Princeton, NJ, 1989), pp. 132, 137; see also Kaplan, *Life,* pp. 310–11. By *impertinent* James meant, 'beside the point', 'not relevant'.

11. The first full-scale attempt to document a war was carried out, a few years later, during the American Civil War, by a firm of Northern photographers headed by Mathew Brady, who had made several official portraits of President Lincoln. The Brady war pictures – most were taken by Alexander Gardner and Timothy O'Sullivan, though their employer was invariably credited with them – showed conventional subjects such as encampments populated by officers and foot soldiers, towns in war's way, ordnance, ships, as well as, most famously, dead Union and Confederate soldiers lying on the blasted ground of Gettysburg and Antietam...

The first justification for the brutally legible pictures of dead soldiers, which clearly violated a taboo, was the simple duty to record. 'The camera is the eye of history,' Brady is supposed to have said. And history, invoked as a truth beyond appeal, was allied with the rising prestige of a certain idea of subjects needing further attention known as realism – soon to have more defenders among novelists than among photographers. ... But the frankness of the most memorable pictures in *Gardner's Photographic Sketch Book of the War* (1866) did not mean that he and his colleagues had necessarily photographed their subjects as they found them. To photograph was to compose (with living subjects, to pose),and the desire to arrange elements in the picture did not vanish because the subject was immobilized, or immobile.

Not surprisingly, many of the canonical images of early war photography turn out to have been staged, or to have had their subjects tampered with. It's now known that the Brady team rearranged and displaced some of the recently dead at Gettysburg: the picture titled 'The Home of a Rebel Sharpshooter, Gettysburg' shows in fact a dead Confederate soldier who was moved from where he had fallen on the field to a more photogenic site.

Susan Sontag, from *Regarding the Pain of Others* (London, 2003), pp. 46–8, 49. The Battle of Antietam (Sharpsburg) was fought on 17th September 1862, with total casualties (on both sides) of 23,000 soldiers killed, wounded or captured; the decisive battle of Gettysburg was fought over 1st–3rd July 1863, with 23,000 casualties on the Union side and 28,000 on the Confederate side killed, wounded or captured. Compare also Sweet, *Traces of War:* 'Here, as in the other representations of the dead at Gettysburg, Gardner's art intervenes in the recording of the image. The corpse has been carried some forty yards and arranged within the frame provided by the stone wall, the musket carefully placed near where it would have been last fired – and yet only by calculating the improbability of the position of the musket could the viewer conclude that this image was arranged' (p. 130; compare also pp. 136–7). It is also the case that the weapon included within this photograph of 'a sharpshooter' is not in fact a sharpshooter's rifle at all, and thus could not have belonged to the dead soldier; although expert knowledge would be required to recognise this.

12. For the Poet, he nothing affirmes, and therefore neuer lyeth. For, as I take it, to lye is to affirme that to be true which is false. So as the other Artists, and especially the Historian, affirming many things, can, in the cloudy knowledge of man-kinde, hardly escape from many lyes. But the Poet (as I sayd before) neuer affirmeth. The poet neuer maketh any circles about your imagination, to coniure you to beleeue for true what he writes. Hee citeth not authorities of other Histories, but euen for hys entry calleth the sweete Muses to inspire into him a good inuention; in troth, not labouring to tell you what is or is not, but what should or should not be. And therefore, though he recount things not true, yet because he telleth them not for true, he lyeth not. ... And therefore, as in Historie, looking for trueth, they [readers] goe away full fraught with falshood, so in Poesie, looking for fiction, they shal vse the narration but as an imaginatiue groundplot of a profitable inuention.

Sir Philip Sidney, from *An Apologie for Poetrie* (c.1580–3; printed 1595); old-spelling text here from G.G. Smith (ed.), *Elizabethan Critical Essays* (Oxford, 2 vols, 1904), Vol. I, pp. 184–5; there are modernised (complete) texts with commentary in K. Duncan-Jones & J. van Dorsten (eds), *Miscellaneous Prose of Sir Philip Sidney* (Oxford, 1973), in G. Shepherd and R.W. Maslen (eds), *An Apology for Poetry, or, The Defence of Poesy* (3rd ed., Manchester, 2002), and in Gavin Alexander (ed.), *Sidney's 'The Defence of Poesy' and Selected Renaissance Literary Criticism* (London, Penguin Classics, 2004), p. 34. Alexander provides (in his Notes, p. 342) a useful clarification of the final sentence in this excerpt. See also F.G. Robinson, *The Shape of Things Known; Sidney's Apology in its Philosophical Tradition* (Cambridge, Mass., 1972).

13. The various instances of truth in fiction that I have examined so far have in common a basis of well-defined and necessarily perceived formal features. All of them are either distinct from verisimilitude or exclude it altogether, since all of them are compatible with indices of fictionality. Moreover, although verisimilitude presupposes things, concepts, or sign systems against which the text may be tested for accuracy, fictional truth spurns referentiality that raises the specter of whether or not the reader acknowledges its accuracy. Instead, fictional truth relies entirely on the text itself as if the latter were self-sufficient. Truth is a modality of text generation.

MICHAEL RIFFATERRE, *Fictional Truth* (Baltimore, MD, 1990), p. 84; compare p. 111: 'Paradoxically, therefore, fictional truth results from two eliminations: first, the suppression or suspension of verisimilitude; and second, the elimination or suspension of the component of time or duration in the narrative. Fictional truth obtains when the mode of the diegesis shifts from the narrative to the poetic.' Riffaterre defines *diegesis* as 'the concrete actualization of narrative structures, namely, the verbal representation of space and time referred to in the narrative and through which it unfolds, as well as the verbal representation of events and characters' (Glossary, p. 127). There is no Glossary definition for 'poetic'.

23

*9 7 8 1 8 4 8 6 1 7 9 2 6 *